Series 561

William
the Conqueror

by L DU GARDE PEACH OBE MA PhD DLitt
with illustrations by JOHN KENNEY

Ladybird Books Loughborough

WILLIAM THE CONQUEROR

For a hundred and fifty years after the time of Alfred the Great, people were continually fighting one another all over England. What the country needed was a strong King who could keep order.

In France there was a young boy, whose name was William, who was the son of the Duke of Normandy. This was the boy who in the year 1066, came and conquered England.

When William was only eight years old his father died. For years he had to remain hidden, because there were men in France who wished to kill the young boy and steal the country and the castles which had belonged to his father.

The Duke Robert of Normandy was the cousin of King Edward the Confessor of England, and when William was twenty-four years of age he came to this country to visit his kinsman.

When William saw what a green and pleasant country England was, he thought he would like very much to be its King. So he persuaded Edward to promise him the crown.

This was something which Edward had no right to do, because in those days, the King was chosen by a council of wise men. It was very unlikely that they would agree to choose a French Duke to be a King of England, but William was already thinking of the future.

At the same time there was in England a young Saxon called Harold and everybody wanted Harold to be the next King.

One day Harold was in a ship which was wrecked on the coast of France. When he and his sailors got ashore they were not treated kindly, as shipwrecked sailors are to-day. They were taken prisoners and put into horrible dungeons.

This was because, at that time, it was considered quite fair to take a man prisoner, and then make his relations or friends pay a lot of money to get him back again. Even an English King, Richard the First, was later held to ransom, as it was called, in this way.

When William heard that Harold had been taken prisoner, he immediately sent for him, and the man who had captured Harold at once brought him to William's castle in Normandy.

William received Harold in a friendly way, and told him how sorry he was that he had been put into a dungeon. He took Harold out hunting, and even conferred upon him the order of knighthood.

All this was in order to get Harold to make the same promise that Edward had made. Harold, of course, wanted to be King himself, but he was really William's prisoner, and he knew that if he did not promise what William asked him, he would never get back to England at all. So he promised to help William to become King of England when Edward should die.

William had not been honest with Harold, because when Harold had made his promise, William had told him to put his hand on a box. Harold did not know that inside the box were some very sacred relics. This meant that if Harold broke his promise, very terrible things would happen to him.

When Harold returned to England, he said that he had only promised because he was a prisoner, and not of his own free will. So when King Edward died, on January 5th, 1066, Harold was crowned King of England in the newly built Westminster Abbey.

William was very angry when he heard this. He was more determined than ever to be King of England himself. So he gathered together all his soldiers to sail across to England and capture it by force.

William the Conqueror was a very clever man. He wanted to make quite sure that his soldiers would be able to land in England, and he was afraid that if Harold was on the beach with a large army, this would not be easy.

So William made friends with a man called Tostig, who was actually Harold's brother, but they had quarrelled, and Tostig had been banished from England. William was sure that Tostig must be very angry with Harold, and would want to be revenged on him.

William was right. So one night William and Tostig sat over a map of England, and Tostig agreed to invade the North of England, a few days before William invaded the South of England. They hoped that Harold would march north to fight Tostig, and William would be able to land without opposition.

In the meantime, William had gathered together hundreds of ships in the French Harbours opposite England. But the late summer gales in the Channel wrecked a lot of the French ships before they sailed, and William's soldiers began to wish they had not so cheerfully engaged to cross the sea and invade England.

It began to look as though all the ships and stores which William had gathered would be wasted, simply because his soldiers were afraid that fortune had turned against them.

Just at that moment a new bright star with a fiery tail appeared in the sky. We know to-day that it was Halley's comet, but William persuaded his followers that it was a heavenly sign, meaning that they would win a great victory over the English.

The appearance of the new star put fresh heart into William's soldiers. They went on board the ships feeling that the invasion of England was under special protection.

It must have been a wonderful sight as William's fleet set out from France. The ships were all brightly painted, with coloured sails, and gay flags fluttering at their mast-heads.

A man whose father saw them sailing across to England wrote: " I heard my father say that there were seven hundred ships, less four, when they sailed from St. Valerie, and there were, besides these ships, boats and skiffs for the purpose of carrying the arms and harness."

You may be sure that there were plenty of anxious men watching on the Kentish cliffs. Everyone knew that William had gathered together an army and hundreds of ships for the invasion of England. But no one knew exactly when he would come.

Harold had also gathered a large army. For many weeks they had been waiting, ready to stop William's men from landing. But now Harold had marched north to York with all his men, to fight Tostig. William's plan had succeeded.

So when the watchers on the cliffs saw the hundreds of ships coming, all they could do was to send messengers galloping away on horses to warn Harold and his army in the far North.

Harold had meanwhile won a victory against Tostig at Stamford Bridge near York. Tostig and the King of Norway, who had come to help him, were both killed in the battle, and Harold and his soldiers were resting and tending their wounds after the fight.

Harold knew, of course, that William's army might land on the south coast at any moment. As soon as his weary soldiers were rested, he would have to retrace his steps down the long road to Kent.

What Harold did not know was that a messenger was galloping through the night to tell him that William's army was already on the way.

William landed on the coast of England without anyone trying to stop him. He must have smiled to himself at the thought of Harold's army far away in the North.

It must have been a very busy sight on the beach near Pevensey when all the horses and soldiers were coming ashore.

First came the archers, with their bows and arrows ready to shoot at anyone who came against them. Then the knights, in full armour, ready to mount their horses and charge the enemy.

But there was no enemy. Only a few watchers high up on the cliffs.

As William himself landed, he tripped and fell. His followers thought this was a bad sign, but William stood up with both hands full of sand and earth. " Look," he said " I have seized England with my two hands."

The Normans were now safely ashore in England. But they knew that Harold's army would be marching south to fight them. The first thing they had to do was to build a fort, inside which they would be safer than on the open beach.

We are told by the man whose father saw them, how William and his knights consulted together and decided where to build the fort. This was easy, because William had brought with him everything that was needed.

Hundreds of carpenters came from the ships, with all the separate parts of the fort, ready made. Instead of nails there were barrels full of wooden pegs made of hard oak, to fasten the parts together. Before nightfall, the fort was finished.

Up in the North of England, Harold lost no time. As soon as the weary messenger had told him that William had landed, Harold ordered the trumpets to be sounded. Within a few minutes the tired soldiers were on their feet again, ready to begin their long march.

Harold and his knights had horses, but most of the soldiers had to march all the way from York to the south coast. This took them many days, and by the time they got there, William had made ready to fight them.

He had done something else. He ordered all his ships to be drawn up on the beach, and had told the carpenters to bore holes in them, so that they would not float. His men knew that they had either to win or die. They could not get back to France.

The battle of Hastings was fought on October 14th, in the year 1066. This is one of the most important dates in the history of England.

Harold and his men stood close together at the top of the hill using their shields to stop the arrows of the Norman archers.

They beat off William's first attack and the left flank of William's army turned and rushed down the hill, with some of Harold's men following.

William saw what was happening and ordered his knights to surround and kill these men.

Then the Normans attacked again and William's horse was killed. Quickly word spread that William was dead, and his men began to move back down the hill. But William took another horse and lifted his helmet so that everyone would see him and know that he was alive.

Then the Norman archers began firing their arrows high in the air. Soon the arrows were falling thick and fast and Harold and the men who remained with him could not stop them all with their shields.

A crowd of Norman knights fought their way up the hill to where Harold was fighting bravely.

An arrow struck Harold just above the right eye.

Then the band of knights burst through the ranks of soldiers and killed him with their swords.

With the death of their brave leader, the English knew that the battle was lost.

After the fighting was over, no one knew which of the dead soldiers was Harold. His friend, Edith Svanneshals, was brought to the battlefield and she recognised him.

There exists today a wonderful picture, called the Bayeux Tapestry, showing the invasion of England by William and the battle of Hastings.

The first thing William did after winning the battle, was to march to London. There were no longer any English fighting men to bar his way, and soon he reached the gates of the city.

William expected to find the gates closed, but instead of this, he was met by the bishops and nobles. They knew that they could not stop William from conquering the whole of England, so they asked him to be King of England without any more fighting.

William accepted, and in a very old book, written at the time, it is recorded that he promised to be a kind lord to the English people. Most of the time William kept that promise.

So a Norman Duke became King of England.

William decided that he would be crowned at Westminster, in exactly the same way as Harold had been. He wanted people to think of him as a true English King, and not as a foreign conqueror.

So on Christmas Day, in the year 1066, William of Normandy rode through the streets of London to his coronation. It was snowing hard, and the streets and houses were white, but we can be sure that all the people came out to see what the new King looked like.

Inside the Abbey, William was crowned by the Archbishop of York on one side, and a French Bishop on the other. As the crown was put on his head, all the nobles shouted. Unfortunately the Norman soldiers outside thought that a riot had broken out, and many people were killed before order was restored.

There stands in London to-day a building which will always remind us of William the Conqueror. This is the Tower of London.

This great keep was built by William on the place where, long before, the Romans had built a fort. Its purpose was to protect London. But it had also another reason. William was never quite sure whether the English people would not rise against him. In the Tower of London, guarded by his soldiers, he knew that he was safe.

The part of the Tower of London built by William is the central keep. It is called the White Tower because of the whiteness of the stone, which William caused to be brought all the way from Caen, in Normandy.

William believed that it was the duty of a King to see that the government of the country was properly carried out. In those days there was no Parliament, as we know it to-day. The King had one or two men to advise him, but he had to do most of the work himself.

William worked hard. He often acted as a judge in the court of law, and wherever he went he was always trying to find out what people thought, and what they wanted.

He was harsh to those who broke the law, but he was always ready to change a law which he thought was unjust.

There were, of course, still people in England who did not like being ruled by a foreign King.

In the North of England there were many such people. Several times William had to march all the way from London with his army, to put down rebellions.

Then came the destruction of York. The men of Northumbria killed the Norman Governor and all his soldiers. Once more William brought his army to restore order.

This time he determined that he would put an end to it. He ordered his men to burn every house and destroy everything they could find, between the Humber and the Tees. This part of England remained a wilderness for more than fifty years.

William devastated the north to prevent further rebellion. He also cleared a large part of the south of England for another reason.

William was very fond of hunting. In those days wild deer, and even wild boars, were to be found in England.

William decided that he would set aside a part of his new kingdom as a hunting ground. He marked out an area nearly a hundred miles round, lying between the River Avon and Southampton Water, containing more than fifty parishes. Then he sent his men to pull down all the houses and churches and villages, and drive away all the people who lived there. This was one of the occasions on which William broke his promise to be a kind lord.

The area which William cleared remains to-day as the New Forest, in the County of Hampshire.

In the clearing of the New Forest, William was thinking only of his own pleasure, not of the welfare of his people. But in many ways William was a wise man and a good King.

One of the things which he did was to order that a great book should be made of all the land and all the people living in England. This had never been done before.

So William sent parties of men in all directions telling them to ask everybody about their land and their houses, their farms and their cattle. With each party was a man who could read and write, and all the answers were carefully written down.

This book exists to-day, and can be seen in London. It is called Domesday Book, and is exactly as it was written, nearly nine hundred years ago.

William the Conqueror, now called William I, was the first real King of all England.

By means of the Domesday Book he knew exactly where everyone lived, and how much property they owned. This meant that for the first time in the history of England, it was possible to ensure that all the people paid their correct taxes to the King.

And by the means of the castles which were built all over the country by his Norman knights, William was able to keep the King's peace.

All this took a long time to do, but it meant in the end that after more than six hundred years of fear and uncertainty, the people of England were once more able to live their lives and work at their trades in safety.

Series 561